As President I Can Save America

When I die don't throw me a funeral. Mourn on your own time. All the laughs and smiles I have given everyone with all the pain I have endured. I deserve a parade.

Table of Contents

Code of Conduct

This will be known in history as the Code of Conduct Address. We need a commander in chief that will choose the people instead of appeasing other politicians. The moral compass of politicians will be tested but the vast majority of this address is for my people, the American people. If elected President, I believe I can save America. It's no secret that America faces many problems now and will face more problems in the future. The only secret that America has in it is that I believe I can solve 50 percent of the problems in 8 years (two full terms). I believe right now even as young as I am at 25 years of age, I have an understanding of America. I've traveled all over the country. I've met thousands of people, I've seen many things already. You must be thinking, who are you to become president? What makes you think you can hold the most important and prestigious job in the world? To answer that, I can say I'm truly a man that represents what becoming president stands for. Hell if Donald Trump could be president why couldn't I? I believe being president you have a duty to every citizen in the county to treat as family. To keep every citizen safe and help improve their lives in every way possible. I believe the president is a man of the people, which I am. I am no extraordinary human being. I'm not a valedictorian, I didn't graduate from college with honors or anything like that. But I'll tell you what, I've lived in a happy two parent home for the first six years of my life. Coming home off the bus to see two loving parents along with your siblings waiting for you. I've lived in a broken home for the rest of my days, where I have one parent I stay with who's trying to play the role of both parents even though my father picked me up on the weekend. 5 whole days without a father in the home is not the same. A single parent home life wasn't something I knew how to adjust to. So at first I was hurting people verbally, getting in trouble and not doing my school work at every turn because I knew trouble meant I would see my father. I've been the guy who fought all the time at the slightest hint of disrespect because of my immaturity and own insecurities. I definitely remember the first time I got hit across the jaw. I went 20 fights in a row without a scratch on my pretty face. Until my 21st fight happened and that's when I realized I wasn't as invincible as I thought. I tried being a creative, by pursuing a music career, I had tons of fun, met a lot of new people but I struggled mightily due to financial reasons. My music was good but my pockets, not so much. I've opened businesses, some failed, some succeed beyond the first year and I still have them today.

I've been broke beyond my wildest imaginations and I've had times where I woke up and saw more zeros in my bank account than I believed possible. I've been the kid that was lying for his friend to the bitter end until my friend's mom came into the principal's office and ended the whole shabang. I've been the frustrated football star of a team behind the scenes where I wanted to lash out but knew the better of it. Even though I was on the field scoring touchdowns, behind the scenes there were a lot of things I didn't agree with and wanted to express it destructively. Ultimately I didn't. I'm also no stranger to danger. I was outside in my neighborhood late, a few guys up the street started shooting and I had to cover my Bestfriend's pregnant cousin to make sure she wasn't hit. I've had fight or flight moments all my life. I know what it's like to be that nerd in class because in high school I was accepted into the National Honors Society. I also know what it's like to have my heart broken. I've been cheated on. It's hard to believe I know I know. But in all seriousness, I've felt that pain in my heart so much that it feels like nothing will ever get better. This sucks and I will never trust another person again. I also know what it's like to be a new parent. To have helped breathe new life into another human being. Knowing you are mainly responsible for their well being, the roof over their head, how mannered they are, leading them in the right direction and protecting them. There is nothing that compares to the very first time you hold your child after birth. A new chapter and a new life to celebrate. The mysteries of what they are going to sound like, who are they gonna look like more? Ahh well I hope my child is a nice person, you can't wait to enjoy your new family. I've also been on the bad end of a birth where the child doesn't make it. To make a long story short, the point is I've personally been each and every one of you. And since I've been each and every one of you I believe that will help us to connect with one another. My past is complicated, however America's past is complicated as well. Sometimes It's not about where you've been but instead about where you're going. Instead it's about the path that you're on right now. America is split into two separate halves. People who are hurting and people who are healing. Right now the vast majority are hurting, there's too many people hurting and not enough of us healing. I intend to be the bridge that closes that gap. The first order of business is reestablishing the value of family. Somewhere along the way we didn't forget about family but we devalued the concept of family. We need every age group to realize how much of a difference it makes growing up in a stable two parent household.As parents sometimes we have to make sacrifices and work through problems with a significant other if the situation is tenable when a child is involved and has many benefits. Because if you break it off with your child's mother or child's father and end up getting a new woman or a new man you're going to run into mostly some of the same problems just with a different person. The benefits of growing up in a stable two parent household can not be denied. Not only for the child but for you too as well. For starters it allows for stress to be taken off of each parent by lessening the amount of responsibilities each one has to account for.

Which then allows the adults to focus more on raising and grooming the children in the house and not have to work 65 hours a week to make ends meet. A more present, more engaged parent leads to a more responsible young adult. Which then leads to better leaders, better politicians, better role models, better workers and ultimately helps us create a better and safer society. Being present will allow parents to focus on reaching a child what's important in life. We as a people forgot that teaching isn't just for when your children go to school. Teaching starts at home. Lesson one used to be how to treat people, how to be respectful of your elders. Lesson one not to mean mug every person you see because they are a stranger. In 2023 the United States was ranked number one in the world in violent crimes according to statista.com. What that tells me is that we have a lot of growing up and healing to do. I guarantee you at least half of the violent crimes from last year could have been diffused rather quickly if someone would have been the bigger person. No amount of police presence, no amount of jail time is going to stop crime in half in this country. Everyone has to look at themselves in the mirror and make a commitment. The problem here in America is internal. That's why it's important that we start to address these problems in every individual home in America.

Internal Affairs

No matter what house we live in. Whether we live in housing provided by the government, or if you live in a mansion, if you're temporarily in a halfway house, you have yourself an apartment, if you're in college in a college dorm, a trailer, an RV or a boat. Emotional trauma doesn't get fixed sitting in a jail cell. Emotional trauma gets dealt with with a therapist or with your loved ones. Pain from emotional trauma that never heals turns into hidden uncontrollable rage. It can turn any innocent into a short tempered man or woman. Which leads to more violence in our country. We need to be proactive when dealing with trauma. As a people we need to be made aware of how important it is to start businesses. Not only so you can see your dreams come true, so that you can create jobs along the way that can help others in their times of need. We need more American made businesses to thrive to help improve the way of life around here for all of us. Like I tell my grandmother when she makes my favorite peanut butter chocolate chip cookies. The more the merrier. Many people are unaware of the programs and tax benefits that make it easier for small business owners. I intend to put things in place to help educate all of the entrepreneurs on the come up. I'll be teaching what I know about the business world and highly encouraging other qualified members of congress to help teach what they know as well. We all share the same duty as one another. To help our fellow citizens in any way we can. Even if it's the smallest piece of information. It could be helping someone with their way around a new city. It could be giving a hot meal to a homeless person. It could be carrying a mature person's bags to their car from the grocery store. Or you could say good morning to someone with a smile. A little kindness can go a long way. One thing internally I think as a country we struggle with is ego. Our heads get too big for our own good. Ego is always the downfall of a great power. Ego drives division where unity is supposed to be. Now one group or a few people refuse to come together with the others for the greater good out of spite. Because they aren't the ones getting credit, trust me if you do the right thing history will forever be on your side. We may have checks and balances in government, but we all need to check our ego everyday before we leave our front door. Once we get rid of ego and cynicism not only in politics but in the rest of society as well we can get back to a path that focuses on unity. The only way we can create a better society for us and for the children of the future is through more unity. With a history rippled with division, the rest of our history moving forward should be led by unity. Which means we don't bully or judge someone for the way they live life as long as they aren't hurting someone. Which means that we aren't damning people and stereotyping people for past events that involved people that look like them. Unity doesn't call for chastising, unity only calls for encouragement and support. I think we all can agree unity breeds bonds of family. That's what I'm here to do. I'm here to re-establish many things, however none greater than the American family. No matter what your family looks like, no matter how many mix of races are in your family, we as a country need to re-establish the family in value. And with family, by blood or not but especially by blood we can't treat someone like they mean nothing and expect them to be there for you all the time. The days of trying to take advantage of these bonds will be over by the time I'm done with my presidency. We need to become more self-sufficient and more self dependent so that we strengthen the family. Not burden the family. Family is more important to our society and democracy than a lot of us realize. The visions of a world that we would want our families to grow up in shape the very principles of our democracy we have today.

I believe a bunch of *I did it all on my own*, *I don't need anybody* and *Family is forever no matter what.* Kind of dragged the essence of families in America down. I'm gonna deliver a shocker here. The real truth to success is that no one does it alone. No matter how much someone screams they did it all by themselves they are lying. There are people that help you along the way. I was always told as a young man it's not what you know, it's who you know. The only thing they forgot to add to that was … *and if you can afford them.* Don't be naive. Don't act like you're too good for something. Sometimes things don't happen organically without money. The saying goes, "Money *talks."* It's a saying for a reason. Very few are going to mentor you for free. You're going to have to pay. For years I had a few business models that I was able to pocket at least a hundred thousand legally. I would show my family, show them how I did it and they still sought out others to show them the way. I couldn't understand it. However once I started thinking about it, I understood. Once I realized the crisis we are in when it comes to the value of the family and the loss of responsibility to uphold the last name your father or mother gave you, I understood why. We are at a time in society where we treat strangers with more kindness, more compassion, more empathy and more respect than we show to our own family members. While we should continue to be all of that to strangers, we need to also apply more of that to our families. We have less pride in our families now than ever and it starts at the very top with dad. Hey to all the young men out there rushing to get older and wanting to have sex with every pretty lady they see. Save the country, wrap it up. Stop having unprotected sex and stop ejaculating into women you don't see yourself having a family. You get the girl pregnant, you're young, she's young, you both don't know what you want. She wants to try to be a family, you're willing to give it a try. You're not prepared for "dad" life and how you won't be able to just do what you want anymore at a moment's notice. You cheat. You leave and now there's a child who doesn't have their father living in the home. And in a lot of cases the father doesn't show up in their lives at all. According to the Census Bureau's Current Population Survey (CPS), the number of children living with two parents has dropped since 1968, while the percentage living with their mother only has doubled. In 1968, 85% of children under 18 lived with two parents (regardless of marital status); by 2020, 70% did, according to the Census Bureau's Current Population Survey (CPS). I am no stranger to these statistics. I lived in a single parent home most of my life. Growing up I only had one friend that lived in a two parent home, everyone else their father wasn't in the picture. This is destroying our country.

We need to get back to the days of respect, honor and being proud of taking care of your children. We need to take pride in raising young men and women, and not by name only. Any man can be a dad, but it takes a real man to be a father. To all the men in the world, not just young men, yes I know life throws temptations at you. But you've got to stop yourself and or wear a condom. I don't know if anyone has told you so I'm telling you now. Understand the responsibilities that are behind your actions. Not only are you affecting your life, the baby's and the woman you're with but you're also affecting each other's families. This is part of the reason why I say as a country we need to grow up. We aren't following these things and not putting enough emphasis on starting a family the right way is hurting us. A lot of people aren't having these serious talks with their children. It doesn't need to be only a talk, it should be a discussion. This kind of discussion should not only be once, because as each year goes by as an adolescent your views change. Making sure both young women and men understand why condoms are so important. And young men if you choose not to wear protection to know what comes with that if the girl pops up pregnant. Step up. That means you both need to step up and take care of your responsibilities. I don't want to hear anything about *Oh she's trying to trap me.* Boy, grow up. You weren't saying that while you were having sex. Stop it. The bottom line is, you need to take care of your responsibilities. Non Negotiable. If you aren't ready for that then you shouldn't be having sex, let alone unprotected sex. If you guys split and you start looking for the next woman, you are going to go through the same problems you went through with the new woman as you did with the mother of your child and vice versa. Stick it out. Gut it out, think of the child. That's why it's important in the first place to understand who you're having sex with and what it could mean. Unless the situation becomes life threatening, something like that, or someone couldn't control themselves, find a way. Barring anything other than that, find a way. Nothing worthwhile happens overnight, it takes time. Do not run from your responsibilities. Running from your responsibilities gets you nothing except hardships and headaches. In our society we lack honesty. Honesty is a core value that helps us progress as a society every day. We need more honesty from our children, our employers, our parents, our teachers, our doctors, our policemen and women, our contractors, our allies, our citizens and also our government. We need honesty from every person in our country if we are going to make sustainable progress beyond my years. We need to become united as we can in our own country to continue our reputation and status among the leaders of the world.

This next lesson I'm going to get into is one that can be of use to young generations and also older generations. I take great comfort in saying more Americans know about credit than any other time in history before. However, the number of Americans is still far too low. According to Yahoo Finance in 2023 nearly 1 in 3 Americans didn't know their credit score. That is roughly 111 million Americans walking around ignorant about their credit score. That can't happen. Credit used to only be information privy to the wealthy. That ends here today. Whether an individual chooses to utilize credit for the tool it is is up to them. However, the ignorance about it ends today. Credit is a tool that can provide many great things for anyone. It can provide leverage for a young entrepreneur who wants to start a business, it can act as a somewhat breather for families who go a month or two without a job and credit can help support an expedition for research. Credit is too important to our country for over a third of our citizens to not have checked their score. I believe that stems from ignorance. One of the biggest lies ever told in American history is that whenever you check your credit, it messes up your credit score. Lie. It has no impact whatsoever. Growing up now in these times, you will need credit every step you turn. You need credit in many cases to get a car, get an apartment, buy a house, some jobs check credit scores, and anything you desire without the upfront capital saved. Hell, it's hard to buy a phone without the phone companies checking your credit score. Not to say that's a bad thing, but to emphasize how almost everything and anything will be utilizing a credit score. You and I both can imagine as more things become digital that more things will require checking your credit score before doing something. Credit can be a resourceful tool that can help anyone fulfill their version of the American Dream. Just like with anything, with great knowledge comes great responsibility. Credit is not a tool to be abused, whatever you use, use to get ahead and remember, you are obligated to pay this money back. So plan ahead before using. Make preparations to make good on any investment you make. The American Economy revolves around systems and at the center of all those systems is integrity. The underlying belief that everyone is playing by the same rules set by our democracy to ensure a safe and fair outcome for everyone. I have a few more things that deal with the moral, mental and emotional state of our country that I want to talk about. I want to talk about learning how to deal with being nervous, fear and how to deal with it. Many never have any discussion close to this one with an adult or parent. I believe being nervous about something and fear are linked everytime. I believe whenever someone is nervous there is a fear behind it. We all reach a time in life if we live long enough to where we get nervous due to whatever factor which can include trying something new, thinking someone else is better than us at something, death, believing our lover is cheating without proof and so on.

Many times I've found that me being nervous was worse than whatever I was nervous about to begin with. What I've learned is that when you are nervous about something you take time to think about it and once you come to a decision or the decision is made for you? You meet the challenge head on. Being nervous about someone new coming to your job and taking your spot is a fear of being replaced, a fear that you're not good enough. Instead of trying to sabotage someone's arrival, welcome them and learn some more skills. If you had enough skills you wouldn't be lacking in confidence. Being nervous about getting a girl's number is because of your fear of rejection. Instead of having that fear of rejection, have a fear about not ever knowing where a meeting between you and her could end up. You could meet a friend of a lifetime, you could be meeting your wife, you could be meeting a girlfriend of 6 months that may not work out but teaches you a valuable lesson, you could be meeting someone with great connections or you also could be meeting a one night stand to cap off a great vacation. And vice versa. Being nervous about someone stealing your lover from you is because of not being able to trust your partner but also because of a fear of being alone. Hey if the person you're exclusively dating is seeking others when both of you were on the same page then… Hey, good riddance. They lost. Move on. Being nervous about telling the truth is a fear of meeting retribution for your actions because you know what you did is wrong. Look I've been there too, it's better to tell the truth and clear your conscience. A clear conscience is something that can not be bought and a peace that can not be achieved by false deeds. You can't steal someone's tractor then a year later run into some big money and buy the person you stole a tractor from and that takes away your guilt. That is a false deed. That is not you gifting them or giving back to your community. That is you trying to mask the guilt you feel inside with the new resources you've obtained. Yes it may replace the tractor you stole but you have no idea what you've done could have done to them mentally. The sleepless nights worrying someone is watching their home. The sleepless nights worrying about if they can trespass on your land and do that then what else can someone do? I would like you to not have stolen the tractor in the first place but tell them the truth and still buy them the tractor. Confidence is another thing that we misdiagnose in this country. Any hint of confidence from another person, people secretly envy them for it and call them arrogant. It's okay to have confidence. Don't let someone else's success and confidence intimidate you. We have to stop that. We haven't been taught how to deal with these things. Instead of feeling jealousy, instead of planning to rob someone of what they have and what we see. We need to learn how to be motivated by others' success and not muster up such jealousy because you don't have what someone else has. They worked hard to be where they are at. If you want what they have you need to work harder, not try to take it from them. Because truth be told, the sauce can't be sold. Meaning you could take what they have but chances are, whatever you took isn't going to set them back for long because if you earned it once, you can earn it twice. So you'll be stuck with some outdated version of whatever you took and not long after they'll have whatever that something was but bigger and better. The game is told, not sold.

Most of us didn't have an adult teach us growing up that greed won't get you anywhere. You can be told something and not be taught it. A lot of us still think being told something means you were taught it. False. I can't say it enough. False. Greed does nothing but get you caught up. Sooner or later your luck will run out, and it's more likely that it'll be sooner than later. As a parent myself I understand that the days of whooping your kid to the point of oblivion are no more and for good reason. Some of the things some of us had to grow up with could be less described as discipline and more as abuse. The times of old are traumatizing and breed some of the things that hold us back with the relationship with our parents as well as our country. I believe in our subconscious mind, the cycle of doing something wrong and then physical pain following shortly after is engraved in a lot of Americans' psyche. While I do believe discipline is appropriate to a certain extent, I do believe that it can be damaging us. It's programming in our minds that whenever someone does something wrong, violence needs to follow after. That's wrong. There's a better way and different way than violence every time. You can teach right and wrong without the means of violence, you can instill values in ways that cause mental pulls and tugs that make a person question their actions instead of beating it out of them and yelling they bet not do it again. I know I'm not the only one out there who felt too afraid to talk to your parents or guardians because you were worried about what harm could come to you even if you weren't doing anything wrong. Your parents or guardians don't know any better, they're just parenting their children the way they were brought up. But times are changing. There are alternate methods out there that can instill discipline and teach your children valuable lessons at the same time. Sometimes physical discipline is the way to go but we need to make sure we are not abusing that. We also owe it to our children to make a commitment to implementing methods of teaching right and wrong that don't involve physical pain. No one wants to see or hear their kid crying. However, sometimes as parents we have to do the hard stuff to teach them because that is the responsibility we bear as parents. As a nation we also need to learn to learn ourselves first but more importantly teach our children when someone does something wrong, forgiveness is in order. Forgiveness does not mean holding people accountable, you still do that especially if a crime was committed. I'm talking about forgiveness, we need to make peace with what happened. We need to accept any role we played in what happened, we need to accept that whoever did whatever to us were acting in a manner unbecoming of a decent human being and that we don't owe their sorry asses anymore of our time. You don't have to deal with people that have done you wrong the same way but that doesn't mean you have to create an enemy. A lot of us are walking around with past trauma that walks around with us in society. In order for us to become a better society. One by one, one citizen at a time we have to forgive. We have to let go of that dead weight we've been carrying around and replace it with optimism, replace it with kindness and replace it with a love that can carry generations for years. We have to forgive. Not for whoever did us wrong, but for us.

Forgiving is for us. Not for them. No matter what age you are. It doesn't matter if you're in your 20's, 30's or mature beyond your 80's. We have to learn how to forgive. The beauty about life is that no matter what age you are, you can always learn something new. We can always evolve, we are never too old to learn and we are never too old to make things right. Hey if you try to fix something and the other party is unwilling, hey you did what you could to try to atone for what you did in the present time. All you can do is help them understand that when they are ready to make peace, that you'll be there to atone for what you've done, you'll be there to admit your wrongs and honestly commit to being better to them in the future. As a citizen of the United States of America, I believe we all share a duty to show the public the right kinds of things, whether you're in the media, whether you're in government or even the average citizen. What I mean by *right kinds of things* are instead of a corny meme everyday, maybe once in a while sharing a success story of a young scientist or a local journalist. We need to show off and bring attention to the less flashy things in life and really appreciate those moments because it's the boring, monotonous things that make a country a success. It's the less highlighted things that keep our standard of living up. We can show you football, basketball, soccer and a bunch of sports highlights all day, but a lot of sustainable real advancement in our country comes from the successes of lawyers, doctors, engineers, entrepreneurs, healthcare workers, our factory workers, our teachers and so on. Showing each other the right things could be posting a highlight but then also highlighting how that said individual went back to school and got their degree to finish schooling. Because school and education is just as important as sports, they both play an equal role in our lives. Not everyone can be a sports star but everyone can be a genius if you work at it.. We have to make sure we all understand that education makes the world go round. The more we know, the more we can do. The more we can do, the better we live. The better we live, the more we can offer and so on. Showing the right things doesn't mean diminish the fact that we still need awareness of what's going on around us but this push is so that we don't forget to share the successes of our fellow citizens and not just the stars of a sports team, not just of the music stars and not just of our favorite actors. Instead of sharing something that can be borderline damaging to a community's image, post someone's small success or better yet, post your own. When we are able to put more positive stories out there, more positive things will happen. This is just a smell step that will help us produce a kind of people we all can be proud of.

You know, there's some people that still believe in that type of thing. In this world we get so caught up in becoming an overnight success that we fail to realize success does not happen overnight. No matter what someone else has told you, success takes hard work. Success is what you see after someone has already taken 1,000 baby steps to get them where they are. It takes a bunch of things to get to whatever success looks like for you. You always have to add to what you've already done. There is no looking at what you are doing and admiring it for too long. You sit back, look at what you've done, smile and then start thinking what can I do to make this better. One thing I've learned working in our great country is that each year you need to add something of value to life. No matter how big and no matter how small. There needs to be evaluation every step of the way and at least one thing new you've added to your repertoire, expertise or to your life's assets each year. Year in and year out. I've worked at the bottom of a company, the middle of a company and I've been the CEO of companies. I've worked blue collar and white collar for nearly a decade. No matter what collar or what title you wear. There's always a need for improvement. We need to help our country re-value the little things. We need to get back preaching that it takes baby steps to reach a milestone. Brick by Brick a house is built. There are no shortcuts or skip the hard work button. Every chance you get, you have to add more value. Every chance you get, you need to improve. Improvement comes when you put yourself in uncharted waters. When you do something new. Improvement comes when you challenge yourself, when you're doing something you're not normally used to doing. Improvement happens when you go off script a bit. If you're never uncomfortable in life, you're not growing. You can not stay in your comfort zone and max out your growth. It's impossible. We need our youth to remember the baby steps. This has a lot to do with why some of our youth feel the way they feel. They see people that have some things that they don't and they feel like they're losing in life because they don't have it or can't get it. Ut uh. This is a fault of our own doing. We need to let our children know with hard work and following your intuition in the right moments literally anything is possible. From the time you're born till the day you die, never stop dreaming. I have a lot of youth in my family. Kids, nieces, nephews, cousins and so on. I also still remember what it was like being a kid. With my experience around the youth, being a youth myself I started living out one life rule that helped me more than anything and I started reaping the benefits from this lesson almost immediately. Instead of complaining about whatever your mom, father or guardian wants you to do. The faster you stop complaining and do what they asked you, the better. Even if you don't want to do what they asked you, whether taking the trash out, sitting up with the right posture, cutting the grass, learning how to cook, taking off your hat during class, not instigating things at school, life is a lot easier when you just say okay. Do what they want, respect the leaders in position because the faster you do what they ask of you, the faster you get back to doing whatever you wanted to do in the first place.

21

The Youth

When I realized this, my life got much better considerably faster. When you stop complaining about how things are a drag, you'll find that you'll be able to start enjoying your own time more and more because you'll have a lot more of it. Gain the trust of the adults around you and the more they will trust you with. Such as behaving yourself when they're not around so they'll leave you to it more often. This is one of the best pieces of advice I could ever give a young person under the age of 20. If no one else will say it, I'll say it. We are failing the youth of this country. Things are getting more expensive for them, there's bad and incorrect information being pushed out there everyday, it seems less safe outside and we need to do everything we can to make it right. We need to pay more attention to grooming young people into leaders. We need to stop treating the youth like just damn kids. We need to stop treating the youth like our new competition and we need to start treating them as if they are who we are trying to leave a better world behind for. We are not inheriting from our ancestors, we are borrowing from our descendants. We need to be producing better leaders. Leaders that will be ready and committed to all of America when it's their time. I would like to start an Early Development Presidency's Program that takes 50 young men and women once every 6 months that invites them to the White House to follow the current president around for a day. Let our young men and women get a glimpse into the day to day activity of an active president. They'll meet with the President, have dinner, introduce themselves, why they believe they could help society improve amongst other things. It is my belief that we need to do all we can to prepare the leaders of our future. The better we prepare our youth, the better our future will be. I bring up leaders, why? Because I wholeheartedly believe we have too many of them in prisons. In America we have a prison problem. There, I said it. We have a prison problem. A lot of people end up in prison because they didn't know any better. They weren't taught right and wrong. They weren't taught the code of ethics. I'm not saying they weren't told, I'm saying they were not taught. A lot of people are inmates because they weren't raised properly, they didn't have that guidance in their life that they needed. They had to fight, scratch and manage all of their lives. Instead of being able to enjoy their youth, they are having to make things happen at an age far earlier than they should. Instead of living they're managing. That's where a lot of kids get lost, which then turns into lost adults. There's three types of people in the world: people who shouldn't be in prison, people who aren't in prison and people who should be in prison. There are some people who could've been leaders that are in prison, there are people who aren't in prison living a normal life then on the other hand there are free people who deserve to be in prison. I've been around women my entire life. Six strong women helped raise me. A common problem that I notice in a lot of women through experience in my life is that women do not trust law enforcement. Not because of their own doing or because all law enforcement have proved untrustworthy but because of some of our outdated guidelines and practices. I can't stress enough that we need to build a new bond between law enforcement and our citizens. We need to build trust between the two. That means any grumpies in law enforcement will have to change but it also means that citizens will have to change. There hasn't been trust there and if we are going to create a better future for our loved ones, it starts here. With trust. Not just trust in law enforcement but being able to have trust in family, trust in our justice system and being able to have trust in companies keeping in mind the well being of society. We need to be able to live with trust in our school systems, we need to be able to have trust in healthcare and our elected officials as well.

For the longest time I contemplated on if I could say or not that countrywide the trust in our law enforcement has dwindled over the years. When in fact, countrywide I don't believe there has ever been a time where over 95 percent of the country has believed in law enforcement whether they had a reason to or not to. I believe that's something we need to fix moving forward if we are going to have a bright future. We need to make law enforcement more personable, I think the first words that comes to the minds of most Americans when it comes to law enforcement is *I hope they don't shoot me*. The first emotion that surfaces when you see a cop is fear, when it should be the feeling of safety. Let me give you an example. You're riding on a two lane street, you and a friend. Cruising, listening to music, doing absolutely nothing wrong. Then you see a cop appear sitting in a spot that you didn't notice until now. The first words out of your mouth shouldn't be *Oh shit, it's a cop*. But if we are keeping it real, that's the thought that comes to mind. Right now as a country when it pertains to law enforcement many feel as if it's them versus us. I do not personally feel this way but I understand the feeling. I know what it's like to feel failed at the hands of our justice system. We have to remember, it's not them versus us. It's me versus you. Any member of law enforcement has a very hard job. These people are risking their lives every day to protect our communities. Yes, we all have flaws and we have witnessed many mistakes, over aggressive force, and more than soft punishments to law enforcement. However, at the end of the day if we are going to completely eradicate the injustices within our justice system? If we are going to become one with law enforcement so that we can see them as a pillar of safety and not a gang of blue? We need a few things to happen. We need all citizens and all law enforcement to dismiss the unspoken but thought. Not all cops are bad and not all citizens are looking to do something bad. We need both parties to realize the other is not the enemy. With the country I want to help re-mold and refocus our citizens will behave in a standard that will respect law enforcement more than enough that will allow them to do their jobs in peace. We need law enforcement to do the same. That's the key. Both of us are coming together for the greater good. That's number one. Number two: we need our law enforcement processes to get more thorough. They need to be vetted thoroughly more and regularly personally to make sure they aren't participating in any hate groups. We need better training. Training that gives other officers the proper training to recognize when aggressive force is being used and methods of how they could go to stop it. This also discourages any law enforcement to abuse the power they have knowing that they can't hide behind a wall. We need more events open to the public that our law enforcement are showing up to, interacting with our officers, developing bonds within the community they serve. Number three: when being pulled over, we need citizens not to be so ready to argue and disrespect a leader in the community. On the flip side, we need law enforcement to teach when they pull someone over. Pulling someone over for an infraction is not to punish an individual, not to profile, and not to meet some dumb quota. Pulling anyone over as law enforcement is to teach the driver in the wrong so that we can make our roads safer, one driver at a time. I believe that more than 95 percent of law enforcement are the good guys in almost every situation. It's the smallest of 5 percent that has created a divide in community and law enforcement since the time they were assembled. We need trust on both sides throughout our country. We need to develop more of a countrywide trust because people are afraid to turn people in on crimes. Specifically sexual assault and physical abuse.

For starters, raping, sexually assaulting and physically abusing anyone, needs to be met with swift and unforgiving discipline through our justice system. This should never be happening. It's sad because this has been happening to men, women and children for thousands and thousands of years. Fellow citizens, the country we are trying to build together has no place for these kinds of behaviors. No place. If a woman says no to sex, it means no. If a man says no to sex, it means no. No means no. And for anyone trying sex on a child with or without consent, you are wrong. They are a child, you are an adult, you need to relax. Get someone closer to your own age and stop being a creep. If you are watching your siblings, cousins, nieces or nephews, your neighbor's kid and sickly enough trying to sexually assault them, you deserve to rot in a cell for the rest of your days. Raping women, children and men needs to stop immediately. Stop beating your partner, you're wrong, your kids see it and they grow up not knowing how to receive and give love properly because of what you're doing. Which then can very well lead to a bunch of domestic violence later on in their future as well. How can we build trust with one another if these kinds of things are going on at an alarming rate? And after one of these egregious acts is committed, no one reports it to the police. We need to kill this notion of not wanting to be labeled a snitch or a rat when it comes to domestic abuse, any rape, any sexual assault, any bullying and any other matter that doesn't involve street life and gang activity. By the way, if anyone is in the business of selling illegal drugs and gang activity I advise you to quit while you're ahead. These are not the days of old, the days of making hundreds of millions of dollars and getting away are not happening. For one our intelligence is too great now. Two, we will get someone to turn on you. Snitches are a part of the drug game. If you are naive enough to turn a blind eye to this fact then you will fail miserably. Three, our technology has evolved so much, it's impossible for you to succeed in the drug trafficking, gang banging business. Four, no one has sold drugs illegally or participated in gang activity and ever escaped death or jail. It hasn't happened and never will. Now, we need to kill this notion of being labeled a rat, it's causing people to be scared to speak up when they see things or have done to them that have nothing to do with the streets. A reality where victims are afraid of being judged in any way by the community to the point where they don't report a disgusting act committed to them is a reality where we have failed. I'm sure almost everyone knows at least one victim of sexual assault or domestic abuse who didn't report to the police. Knowing at least one person is the bare minimum. There's various reasons these victims don't report the unforgivable acts committed. To name a few; sometimes they don't know what is happening they're confused, shocked, afraid their wrongdoer will harm them, afraid no one will believe them and also they have doubts that our justice system will serve proper justice. That last reason is something no citizen in America should be okay with. This address should serve as a notice to everybody that plays any role in our justice system that we need to do a better job with gaining the trust of the citizens you serve who help pay y'all with their hard earned tax money. Our justice system needs to investigate all allegations of sexual assault and abuse with top priority.

I believe I can change America by healing America internally. From the inside out. All the pussyfooting and conversations other politicians avoid, I'll meet head on. Now any alien talk is off limits, but other than that I swear I'll tell you as much as I can when I can. I'll share everything I can in my power. The good, the bad and the ugly. I'll tell you one thing. There won't be a lot of ugly with me. But more importantly our country was established on certain values. As President I would like to strengthen those values while at the same time establish new ones for our country. As time keeps going on, as a society we need to evolve. We need our laws to also evolve. Some of the old ones have to be modified, done away with while also creating new ones. The success of America is directly connected to the notion of the American Dream. The American Dream for America born citizens sometimes seems unexciting because of how well we have had it in America for the last 30 years. The life we have lived for the last 30 years is a life of privilege, liberation and opportunity. Our relative peace has some of us jaded in terms of how appreciative of the life we live here are. We've had it so good. But in other countries, it's not like how it is here in our home country. We need to sit back and appreciate the life we have here at home because there are billions of people who would love to be here instead. We are not owed anything. I would like to remind everyone that the truth of the matter is being so far removed from the truth due to time, we don't know everything. But we do know that truthfully that unless you're Native American, our people did not start here. So in a sense we are all immigrants except anyone who was brought over here from slavery. So we must not judge or deny all who seek to come to our country. Our immigrant policy and accepting aliens into this country has always been a heated debate. I don't wanna close anyone out, but I do want to find a way to expedite our immigrant process. We use government money to do everything else. It's time we devote more of our stockpile on that. I want to prioritize making sure our borders are secure so no one can enter our country without being checked out first. We need to help out Texas, all our southern states and the rest of America to combat the influx of illegal aliens. I want to be clear, I don't want to keep anyone out. However before you enter this country, we owe it to our citizens here to make sure people trying to enter the United States go through the proper channels. And they will. If I have to take control of overseeing the whole process myself I will. America and immigrants have always had a special relationship, I'm not trying to deny the continuation of that but we need to do better.

<u>We Are All Immigrants</u>

When I think about the special relationship that we have with immigrants coming to the U.S. legally, I think of Albert Einstein who came to the United States of America from Russia who is universally recognized as one of the smartest men to have ever lived. Who's equation stating energy and mass but in different changed the world. The man who discovered the photoelectric effect and won the Royal Astronomical Society Award. Think of Salma Hayek who came to the United States of America from Mexico. Salma is one of our favorite actors who gave us a great performance in Frida. Salma who continues to support and speak up for Women all across the globe. Being more than an actor Salma was recognized for all she does, in 2001 receiving Glamour Magazine's Woman of the Year Award. Think of my personal favorite, Joel Embiid. Who came to the United States of America from Africa. Joel in his profession has won the most prestigious award available to all players in the National Basketball Association with the MVP Award. The seven-time all star Embiid donated $100,000 to organizations that serve the homeless and youth services. Or think of Madeleine Albright, who came to the United States of America from the Czech Republic. Madeleine showed relentless perseverance throughout her life and political career. Regardless of political party, every woman should be inspired by her story. Madeleine became the 1st woman to hold the position of Secretary of State in the United States. In 2012 Barack Obama awarded Madeleine the Presidential Medal of Freedom. Now not every immigrant turns out to be one of these four, however, let's be clear here, immigrants have always been a part of our history. Immigrants have always been great contributors to our society. As Americans we should take great pride that the country we live in is universally recognized as a sanctum for people who want a fair shot at chasing their dreams. We should take great pride in that and welcome immigrants who seek to become legal citizens. For our foreign policies and aid, I understand a lot of Americans have been confused in why aid is chosen to give to who. Confused about why this amount and also confused as to what the money is going towards. That's one thing during my presidency I look to change for good. I want to develop a system that will allow the President to seek counsel from trusted members in society that keep up with the state of politics. Not members who are dealing with other politicians everyday but actual members in society.

The purpose of this would be to get back some real insight and feel on what the actual public is thinking and will help each President get a better gauge on what the public needs from individuals who deal honestly with the public. The trusted members could be professors, doctors and anyone in society that wants to become a member. There would be vetting, tests, agreed to surveillance to a certain extent to ensure no agendas are being pushed, no home terrorism, and no blackmailing. This position would need anonymity on both sides, no letting people know your position and no one from the government would be allowed to either. None of their opinions or advice would be publicized. I think this private counsel will be great for every president that wishes to have it. It will give each president a different insight into the real public and not just massive points of data and percentages. As A.I. technology advances, I want to stay in touch with the real people of this country every chance I get. I like to think of myself as a hardworking showman. I shine brightest when the lights are brightest and when the lights are shut off I'm in the lab working on my bag as they say. There's a lot to be said about a man or woman in the way they lead and who they surround themselves with. I wasn't fortunate enough to meet either of my grandfathers but if they were anything like me I would imagine they would say: "Assholes are rude but they'll tell you the truth, the nicer they are, the more they lie." That's exactly what I believe, so I like to surround myself with a little bit of both because I believe I am a little bit of both. I can tell hard truths while on the other hand I can say things to make anyone happy for their days. Our government needs a bit of that mix more now than ever. We have a lot of mature men and women all throughout our congress and all of the government. The average age of Members of the House at the beginning of the 117th Congress was 58.4 years; of Senators, 64.3 years according to SpringShare. We have to do something about that. Not that there isn't value in experience and wisdom in maturity but we need to get that number down to mid 40's to low 50's at least. We need to get younger, we need to get fresh, younger faces in our government . I'm not calling for a complete overhaul, I'm talking about a mix of the mature and young. We need to start grooming future politicians and empower them. In our country most young folk are content and we can't be that. Other countries are coming, we need to stay on top of our game with each generation. We need to constantly have new generations of politicians. We need the more mature congressmen and women to mentor younger upcoming men and women interested in the position. Not only once either but many times over. Each member of Congress, each member of the government should have a constant flow of mentees if we truly have a love for our country. We need to take on mentees so our country will have capable leaders after we are gone. 5 mentees every ten years would work wonders for our country. Every mentee should possess certain qualities such as a great work ethic, a healthy nationalism, a healthy level of confidence, great core values, a genuine love for all people and a willingness to learn. Teaching others to do your job just as well as you or even better is never easy. Paying our knowledge forward to the younger generations or anyone looking to have a future in something you have expertise calls for a lot. Mentoring someone calls for us to put our pride aside, drop all egos, forget about our biases, forget about political parties, put skin color aside and family homerism aside. Being a leader isn't just being a leader to your family but being a leader to every person you come across. Even your enemies. Being a leader and a mentor calls for patience. Patience is a virtue and we need to treat it like money. If you don't have it, you better get some. For the betterment of our country now and for the betterment for our country's future. Being open minded, understanding that there is no one right way. There are a thousand ways to do something right. We can't be stubborn to a point where we destroy creativity. We can't tell ourselves, it's only my way or the highway. If that's your way, you have lost before you even began. Life is about the changing variables, we can't afford things to stay the same or regress. New isn't always bad. We need to accept that.

I know I said I was going to speak about the healing and raising of our country but I feel a need to briefly touch on a few things I would like to put in place when I become president. I believe if I put my mind to it, gain some momentum that I can truly become the President of the United States. What I want to put in place for our country, especially for the younger generations, is an hour-long weekly session with me where I go in depth about different topics each week that get taped and uploaded to the Internet for the people to see. I want to find ways to make healthcare more affordable for 1099 workers and entrepreneurs to where if you have life insurance you will get a reduced rate. I want to hold insurance fairs for life insurance to help every citizen in America understand the benefits of each life insurance and also how affordable it could be. How it can protect a family from a lawsuit and injustice. I want to talk to America about the certain types of things we need to be asking for in our policies that cost less than $5 a month that could save you from bankruptcy if a specific problem arises. We need jails and prisons to be less of trying to keep people in cages but more of rehabilitation systems. We need people who are arrested to return to society as close as model citizens as they can be. We don't need them to come back. Our country is better off if we have more productive and good for society citizens free than having confused, trouble making citizens locked up. Of course whoever gets arrested has to want to do better in society but we also have to make it a world where it is easier for them to thrive once they are released. We have to make it easier for them to return to society healthier, smarter, more polite, better at decision making, more considerate of their neighbor and also with the right discipline to be able to get through each day staying on the straight and narrow. If an inmate gets released from prison and isn't able to get a job,l because of their record what do you think they are going to do? Not everyone has a support system to help them during trying times. They are going to go right back to doing what they used to because now they feel as if they have no option because if they can't make money, they won't eat. If they can't make money, they can't afford a place. Yes they did put themselves in that predicament but I know you and I have made mistakes as well. Mostly everyone at the very least deserves a fair shot at a second chance. We need to make sure the conditions in every prison around the country are humane. We need to make sure that we are doing more to get back a productive citizen rather than letting loose a troublemaker destined to come back to prison. That's something I want to emphasize during my tenure and I will pursue the best ways to put policies that will last long after I'm gone. I believe that no one should be able to get away with making a false claim about another citizen either. If whatever you claim is proven to be false you will face consequences for your actions. Right away.

35

If we are to build the country we know we can be we have to acknowledge the lies and build a country foundation based on truth. Starting at every level of life. One thing I want to address is the pay for our healthcare workers and pay for our teachers and professors. These two groups of citizens in large part keep our country running. For decades they have been and are underpaid. I don't believe there is a number that could properly pay our men and women in those services. However, for decades they have been massively underpaid across the board. We have to increase their pay because they are in need of better wages so they are able to work less hours and change personnel more without having to compromise a level of care and without having to compromise their standard of living. We can't say the youth is what we do everything for then the people who groom them while we are away at work, we don't pay well. Ut uh. That's not how that works. I want to implement a system for the top percenters in this country that if you donate a certain amount of money to help underprivileged students financially in their first year of college that they'll receive a special tax break. It's a win-win for everyone involved. I believe helping out the next generations is the best thing we can do. We need to figure out every possible way we can to help them reach their goals. Now for everyday families, one of my goals is to make housing more affordable. Making housing more affordable so that every week you aren't having to take half of your paycheck and putting it aside for a mortgage or rent. I want to be able to get that by only setting aside a fourth of your paycheck and then down to a fifth and so on. The more money in your pocket, quite frankly the more you have to save, and the more you have to save the more you'll be able to spend on upgrading your standard of living. I want to make sure every family knows which tax breaks they can get. I want to make sure every family knows how to get an advantage every day, every year which benefits not only the families but also our government. We need to provide affordable healthcare costs for families. Whether that responsibility falls on the government or the private health companies. Either way I want to make sure we find a way to take care of people when they are sick and also to help citizens maintain their health. The easier we make life for the middle class and poor, the better all of our lives will be. The better off our society will be. We know the rich have what they need and their standard of living is high. Instead of figuring out how to bring the rich closer to the middle class. We need to find ways to bring the poor and middle class up to the rich. Money is not everything, I want to repeat, money isn't everything. Ultimately though, the more money every family has, the less stress there is on the family. Which results in easier times for each family that is able to keep more money in their pockets. The easier it is on families to live in our country, truly live, the better our society will be.

Once again, we need to strengthen the value of family in our country. With that strength in family we will give our young men and women something worth fighting for. We will give the men and women of our country a new found flame to protect. We will reignite our citizens resolve to restrengthen our military. In our history I think you'll find that everytime we call upon our citizens to help defend our country, we always respond. My grandfather served in the war and my grandmother also was a veteran. They spoke only highly of their time serving. They gained brotherhood, sisterhood, more dignity, pride, a newfound respect for their country and also each other. Not only did they defend our country but little did they know that their time in the service would create a family. I come from that. I remember when I was in high school, a recruiter listed all of the benefits: college being paid for, travel, strength and conditioning training, brotherhood, sisterhood, being able to protect yourself and your family, the well deserved pay, protecting our great country and also the allure of being a veteran. There are many benefits of joining any of our military forces including the Navy. Our Navy is beyond impressive beyond belief. However, the world is either caught or is actively catching up. We have made many attempts in the past to develop the most effective battleships in which I share the same desire. But let's face the facts, we haven't been too successful there. I believe it's a simple matter of putting our money in the right places. Instead of trying to go all in on one massive vessel. Let's pump the brakes. Let's put our immediate focus on getting more defensive, lesser vessels out there quickly and efficiently. Then after we add more defensive vessels we will need to take baby steps to improve our latest model and work our way up. I say focus on defensive models more because it's no secret most wars are wars of attrition. Who can outlast the other and who has the resources too? That's the big thing. I have many more strategies to strengthen all of our military forces. I have many plans and big plans to get us where I want us to be. It can only start with conversation. Nothing can or will ever improve without it. If there's something I want everyone to leave with, it's with this message. As a country we need to heal. Once we heal, we need to learn the errors of our ancestors, our own mistakes and we need to learn every tool out there in the universe we can utilize. After we learn as much as we can up to a point because you'll never stop learning and also because smart is "in." Don't worry, the older you get, the more you'll learn that. After we learn, we apply our knowledge. There is no sense in learning if you aren't going to showcase or apply the newly obtained knowledge. After we showcase and apply our knowledge we collaborate with our fellow citizens on how to improve our society. Soon after that, we will start seeing results.

As a country we can't skip any steps. It's like setting out your week at the gym and you skip leg day. Ut uh. That's gonna come back to haunt you. Skipping hard work never breeds success. Skipping hard work never breeds success. Success is never you do one or two things and all of a sudden you're successful at what you want to be successful in. Success is never simple. If it takes that much to be successful as a person, imagine what it takes for a country to thrive and be successful. That is why we need every American citizen and people who are aspiring to be an American citizen to be a star in their role. Everyone has a role. Whatever it is that you're doing, be great at it. Nothing goes unnoticed. There may be no recognition for you being a star in your role but that should be irrelevant if we are doing what we do out of the kindness of our hearts and for the betterment of our surroundings. Last thing before I get you all out of here. For us to improve as a society I have something I want to do with America. If yall do it, I'll do it too. I want everyone to make a checklist. On that checklist I want you to put 10 boxes on there. Put 10 boxes on the page all vertically aligned with space in between each box. Next to the first box I want you to write, *Was I kind today?* Next to the second box I want you to write, *Was I fair today?* By the third box I want you to write, *Was I supportive today?* Next to the fourth box write, *I didn't judge today.* Next to the fifth box write, *Did I make progress today?* Next to the sixth box write, *I wasn't intimidated by the truth.* Next to the seventh box write, *I'm burden free.* Next to the eighth box write, *I helped someone today.* Next to the ninth box write, *Did I think of my "family" today?* Family is whoever you consider to be your family, usually the closest to you. It is not defined strictly by blood. Next to the last box I want you to write, *I voted for Ghazi today.* Before you go to bed I want everyone to go over this checklist and make a mental note of your day. If you check all of these or most of these every night honestly then you should sleep well. You should sleep well knowing that you and I are and will be a part of the solution moving forward. Thank you. I hope to speak to you all again very soon. God Bless you all and God Bless America. Let's shape the future.

<u>Description</u>

It goes without saying that right now as a country we are in delicate times politically. There's more tension now than ever. With seemingly no right answer on how to bring the country together amidst our foreign affairs, I will be the bridge that connects the gap. I will be a president like no other, a president of transparency, communication, life building and honesty. Part of the great divide amongst our people is there's a big absence of family which leads to a lot of people being misguided. There's not enough information out there helping people understand what is expected of a citizen and what a citizen needs to know to thrive in our country. Our duties as men and women start with our family and then next it is to our country which means helping our other citizens in every way we can. I intend to do just that. Raising the standard of each and every American citizen will revitalize patriotism in every citizen to new heights that will bring us together on every issue. I want to bring in the new generation on every front, not to disregard the older generations of leaders but to learn from them then carry on the country with new ideas with precedent in mind. A new generation of leaders in politics, science, technology, military, lawyers, doctors, child care, teachers, entrepreneurs, sports stars, media, etc. As a country we need to reprioritize who we are inspired by. As a country we need to put more emphasis on encouraging our young men and women to go to school for certain careers. We need to reiterate the need for more of everything but in the right way. Being president I understand will be a challenge but we all will be challenged to look at ourselves in the mirror and ask who we really are.

www.ingramcontent.com/pod-product-compliance
Lightning Source LLC
Chambersburg PA
CBHW051716250726
48653CB00007B/3060